HARD NUTS
OF HISTORY
Wars and
Battles

TRACEY TURNER
ILLUSTRATED BY JAMIE LENMAN

First published 2015 by
A & C Black, an imprint of Bloomsbury Publishing Plc
50 Bedford Square, London WC1B 3DP

www.bloomsbury.com

Bloomsbury is a registered trademark of Bloomsbury Publishing Plc

ISBN 978-1-4729-1094-3

A CIP catalogue for this book is available from the British Library.

This book is produced using paper that is made from wood
grown in managed, sustainable forests. It is natural, renewable and
recyclable. The logging and manufacturing processes conform
to the environmental regulations of the country of origin.

Printed in China by Leo Paper Products, Heshan, Guangdong

1 3 5 7 9 10 8 6 4 2

CONTENTS

INTRODUCTION

Wars and battles are only for the hardest hard nuts, and this book contains some of the toughest of the tough, from rampaging generals to risk-taking spies. Some of them were warriors, some fought behind enemy lines, but all of them were as hard as nails.

FIND OUT ABOUT . . .

· A tea party that started a war

· Courageous fighting poets

· The ruthless general who became a peaceful vegetarian

· The sneaky queen who tricked her enemies

If you've ever wanted to parachute into occupied France, sail a Persian warship, or march on Rome, read on. Follow the hard nuts into the muddy trenches of the First World War, across revolutionary Russia, and on to the battlefield at Waterloo.

As well as discovering stories of courage and cunning, you might be in for a few surprises. Did you know, for example, that England had three different kings in just one single year? Or that Leon Trotsky was named after his own prison guard?

You're about to meet some of the toughest hard nuts to ever set foot on a battlefield . . .

Plus take the quiz on page 54 and find out how much you really know about different wars and battles and the people who fought in them.

THE BATTLE OF WATERLOO

In 1789, France had a revolution, in which ordinary people took control of the country, and kicked out the king and queen and the aristocrats, who'd been living lives of luxury while poor French people starved.

HEAD CHOPPING

The French Revolution involved lots of executions using an efficient head-chopping machine, the guillotine. While poor people in other European countries might have quite liked the idea of a revolution, the people in charge of those countries certainly didn't. The European leaders fought against France and its military commander (and later emperor), Napoleon, in the Napoleonic Wars.

BIG MISTAKE

Napoleon fought successfully against the different European armies, but made a big mistake when he tried to invade Russia – hundreds of thousands of French soldiers died, France surrendered and Napoleon was banished to an island. But in true hard-nut style he escaped, marched to Paris and gathered an army. His French army met the allied armies of Europe, led by the British Duke of Wellington and the Prussian general Blucher, at the Battle of Waterloo in Belgium, where Napoleon was defeated.

THE DUKE OF WELLINGTON

HARD NUT RATING: 8.3

Wellington joined the British Army two years before the French Revolution began, and straight away set about getting himself a reputation as a brilliant general and all round tough nut. He fought in India and in the Peninsula War, in which Britain supported Portugal and Spain against Napoleon and revolutionary France. By the time he met Napoleon at Waterloo in 1815 he'd been made a Duke, and was famous for his brilliant military tactics.

NOBBLING NAPOLEON

At the Battle of Waterloo, things started off well for the French – their army was bigger, until reinforcements arrived for the allied army (which included British, Dutch, Belgian, German and Prussian troops). But although the battle was close, the allied armies finally put a stop to Napoleon, who was exiled to an island again (a much more remote one this time), where he died in 1821

PRIME MINISTER WELLINGTON

After his victory, which was seen as a triumph of Wellington's clever battle tactics, Wellington was more popular than ever. Waterloo was his last battle, though. After that he entered the world of politics, and became the British Prime Minister in 1828.

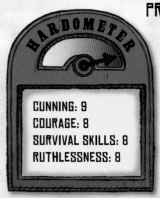

HARDOMETER

CUNNING: 9
COURAGE: 8
SURVIVAL SKILLS: 8
RUTHLESSNESS: 8

THE GREAT ROMAN CIVIL WAR

The Great Roman Civil War was fought between Julius Caesar and Pompey the Great.

CAESAR TAKES CHARGE

When Caesar got the top job of Consul (a bit like Prime Minister) in 59 BC, he made an alliance with Pompey (because he was a military tough nut) and Crassus (because he was extremely rich). With his powerful mates, Caesar got more power than was usually allowed. After his time as Consul, which was limited by law, he was made governor of various parts of the empire, with command of a whopping great army that he used to conquer Gaul (modern-day France and Belgium) and invade Britain.

STRUGGLE FOR POWER

However, the three-man alliance didn't last: Crassus was killed, and Caesar and Pompey began a struggle for power. The Roman government (the Senate) backed Pompey, but Caesar was popular with the ordinary people of Rome because of his conquering exploits. The Senate demanded that Caesar give up his army or become an enemy of Rome. In reply, Caesar marched his army from Gaul across the Rubicon River into Italy: this meant civil war. He marched on Rome, while Pompey ran away. The civil war lasted four years, from 49 to 45 BC.

JULIUS CAESAR

POMPEY THE GREAT

Pompey made his name as a tough Roman general: he reconquered Spain, helped crush Spartacus' slave rebellion, stopped pirates menacing the Mediterranean and conquered more land in the Middle East.

HARD NUT RATING: 8.8

GOODBYE ROME

After his major falling-out with Caesar and Caesar's march on Rome, Pompey decided there was no point in meeting Caesar to fight for Rome, and ran off to central Italy. Caesar battered Pompey's troops in Spain, and took control of Rome. Then he went looking for Pompey.

BATTLES AND BEHEADING

Pompey met Julius Caesar at the city of Dyrrachium, in what's now Albania. Pompey was besieged, but managed to break out and defeat Caesar's troops, who fled. But Pompey's victory didn't last long. At the Battle of Pharsalus Caesar beat Pompey's army, despite having fewer troops. Pompey ran away to Egypt, which wasn't a good move: the Egyptian leader, Ptolemy, chopped off his head. Caesar ruled Rome until 44 BC, when he was assassinated.

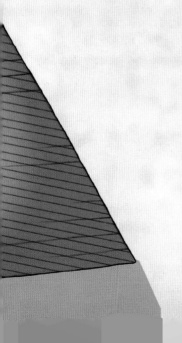

HARDOMETER

CUNNING: 9
COURAGE: 9
SURVIVAL SKILLS: 8
RUTHLESSNESS: 9

THE RUSSIAN CIVIL WAR

In 1905 people revolted against the unfair system in the Russian Empire, and Tsar Nicholas II made promises he didn't keep. In 1917, there were food shortages, around 1.8 million Russians had been killed in the First World War, and the winter was especially harsh. The cold, hungry Russian people had had enough: they rioted, and were joined by government troops. The Tsar gave up his crown, and a new government was formed. In October of the same year, another revolution put a group called the Bolsheviks in charge.

BOLSHEVIK TROUBLE

Russia left the First World War, but the fighting wasn't over: civil war broke out between the Bolshevik Red Army and the White Army, made up of people who disagreed with the Bolsheviks, and troops from Britain, France and America who didn't like the Bolsheviks either. Leon Trotsky took charge of the Red Army and won the civil war in 1921.

LEON TROTSKY

HARD NUT RATING: 8

Lev Davidovich Bronstein was born in 1879 in Ukraine, which was part of the Russian Empire at that time. He had strong ideas about getting rid of the Tsar and making things fairer, and was exiled to Siberia for his views. But in 1902 he escaped his freezing prison with a passport in the false name of Leon Trotsky – the name of his prison guard!

REVOLUTIONS

Trotsky's new name stuck. He travelled to London, where he met fellow revolutionary Lenin, and came back to Russia for the 1905 revolution, when he was arrested again, and again made a daring escape! This time he stayed out of Russia until 1917 – in time to organise the October Revolution with Lenin and the rest of the Bolshevik party.

RED VS WHITE

Trotsky led the Red Army in the Civil War that followed, and killed anyone who opposed it. The Red Army, a united, determined fighting force thanks to Trotsky, eventually beat the White Army, which wasn't as united or organised. The Civil War claimed millions of lives, more due to disease and starvation than to fighting. Trotsky won the war, but ended up being chucked out of the new Soviet Union by its new leader, Stalin. He was killed in Mexico in 1940 by an assassin sent by Stalin.

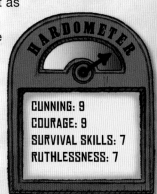

HARDOMETER

CUNNING: 9
COURAGE: 9
SURVIVAL SKILLS: 7
RUTHLESSNESS: 7

THE PERSIAN WARS

The Persian Empire began with conquering toughie Cyrus the Great, and gradually became bigger and more powerful. By 499 BC it covered land stretching from the Mediterranean Sea all the way to the Indus valley (where the modern country of Pakistan is now), including some Greek islands. The Persian Emperor, Darius the Great, wanted the rest of Greece too.

INVASION

Darius invaded and the Persian Wars began, between the Persian Empire and united city-states of ancient Greece. The wars were fought during the reign of two Persian emperors: Darius the Great and then his son, Xerxes the Great. Even though the Persian Empire was big and powerful, it never managed to defeat ancient Greece.

Lots of hard nuts fought in the Persian Wars, but one of them, who fought in the naval Battle of Salamis, was unusual as well as tough . .

QUEEN ARTEMISIA

HARD NUT RATING: 8.3

Artemisia was Queen of Halicarnassus, in what's now Turkey, which was part of the Persian Empire. When her husband the king died, she ruled on her own. In those days, two and a half thousand years ago, it was very unusual for a woman to be in charge.

XERXES THE GREAT

Persian Emperor Xerxes the Great had already tried invading Greece in 490 BC, but it hadn't worked out very well. Ten years later he was ready to try again, this time by sea. He called the commanders of his fleet together, including Artemisia. Artemisia was the only woman, and also the only commander who thought the invasion was a bad idea, but Xerxes ignored her wise advice.

SNEAKY ARTEMISIA

Artemisia sailed her fleet of five ships into the Battle of Salamis with the rest of the Persians. She fought bravely but also sneakily – she flew the Greek flag to confuse the enemy. Xerxes thought she was his best commander, but he should have listened to her advice because the Persians were battered by the Greek ships. The Greeks celebrated their victory, but they were absolutely livid about Artemisia – the thought of a woman commanding ships and fighting them sent them into a blistering rage. Although they tried, they never succeeded in capturing her.

HARDOMETER

CUNNING: 8
COURAGE: 9
SURVIVAL SKILLS: 8
RUTHLESSNESS: 8

THE BATTLE OF THE LITTLE BIGHORN

In the 1800s, the United States government began forcing Native Americans to live in 'reservations', so that the government could take the land that used to be theirs. The government was especially keen on Native Americans clearing out if, for example, they discovered gold on their land. Some Native Americans put up a fierce resistance as they were pushed off their land.

GOLD

The Sioux people had been promised that they could always live in the Black Hills of Dakota, but when gold was discovered there the government first tried to buy the land from them, then tried to force them off it and into small reservations. The result was the Battle of the Little Bighorn in 1876, where the Sioux banded together with the Cheyenne and the Arapaho tribes into a 3,000-strong force, under the leadership of Chiefs Crazy Horse and Sitting Bull. At the battle the United States suffered its worst defeat in the war against the Native Americans.

GENERAL CUSTER

HARD NUT RATING: 8.3

George Armstrong Custer was born in 1839 in Ohio. He went to military school and graduated in 1861, just in time for the American Civil War (see page 38). By the end of the Civil War Custer was in charge of a division of cavalry, and was well known for his bravery. After the war he stayed in the army, fighting against the Native Americans.

TROUBLESOME SIOUX

Custer was sent to sort out the resistant Sioux people, and led his 600 troops through the mountains to the Sioux camp at Little Bighorn. Instead of waiting for reinforcements, and although the soldiers were tired from their march over the mountains, Custer divided the men into three groups, and led the men in his charge against the Native Americans. But Custer had seriously underestimated his enemy: he was hugely outnumbered. Crazy Horse, Sitting Bull and their warriors were experienced and determined. Custer and all the men in his charge were killed, including two of Custer's brothers. The Native Americans had won the battle, but they ended up losing the war, and most of their land.

HARDOMETER

CUNNING: 7
COURAGE: 9
SURVIVAL SKILLS: 8
RUTHLESSNESS: 9

THE FIRST WORLD WAR

The First World War was sparked when the heir to the Austro-Hungarian Empire was assassinated in Serbia in 1914. Austria-Hungary declared war on Serbia, and the powerful countries in Europe took sides. The war was the biggest in history up to that point: over 65 million people fought in it, and around 18 million died.

TAKING SIDES

On one side, Germany, Austria-Hungary and the Ottoman Empire became known as the Central Powers. The other side, the Allies, included France, Russia, Britain and Serbia, and as the war went on other countries joined in, including the United States. The British Empire was vast, so soldiers from different parts of it – India, Canada, the West Indies, South Africa, Ireland, Australia and New Zealand – joined in the fight on the Allies' side too.

WORLD WAR

Most of the war's battles were fought on the Western Front – a battle zone that ran from the Belgian coast down through France to the Alps mountain range. The new weapons of war were so destructive that soldiers dug

trenches to shelter from the impact of huge guns. Battles raged in other parts of the world as well: Germany and Austria-Hungary fought Russia on the Eastern Front, and in Serbia until Serbia was defeated in 1915, and the Allies fought the Ottoman Empire in the Middle East. There was also fighting in far-flung parts of Germany's and Britain's empires.

BLOODY BATTLES

The battles of the First World War are remembered as some of the bloodiest in history. One of the best known is the Battle of the Somme, which lasted from 1 July 1916 until November 1916. On the first day of the battle, 20,000 British soldiers died and another 40,000 were wounded. By the end of the battle, 125,000 British were dead, 204,000 French, and a huge number of Germans – possibly as many as 680,000.

END OF THE WAR

In 1918, the Central Powers made a last-ditch attempt to break through the Allied lines on the Western Front but were forced back. The Allies had won, and the fighting finally ended on 11 November 1918.

Millions of people were involved in the First World War – turn to page 24 and 26 to read about a few of them.

FLORA SANDES

Flora Sandes was one of only two British women who fought in the First World War. Lots more women were involved in the war – making weapons in factories, driving ambulances or nursing – but Sandes was actually on the battlefield.

HARD NUT
RATING: 8

JOINING UP

Flora Sandes was 38 when the First World War broke out. She joined the St John's ambulance service and went to Serbia, where there was fierce fighting. At first she worked with the ambulance service, but then she enrolled in the Serbian Army along with a few other Serbian women. Sandes was badly wounded by a hand grenade, and was awarded a medal for bravery and gained a promotion to Sergeant Major. After the war she was made a Captain. Because of her injuries she couldn't fight any more, but ran a hospital instead. Sandes got married and lived in France and then in Belgrade (now in Serbia), where she drove Belgrade's first taxi. She lived until 1956.

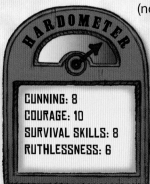

HARDOMETER

CUNNING: 8
COURAGE: 10
SURVIVAL SKILLS: 8
RUTHLESSNESS: 6

SIEGFRIED SASSOON

HARD NUT RATING: 7.5

Sassoon enlisted in 1915, aged 27, as an officer in the Royal Welsh Fusiliers in the British Army, and was sent to fight in France on the Western Front, where he fought in the Battle of the Somme in 1916. His bravery in battle earned him the nickname Mad Jack.

WAR POEMS

Sassoon was already a published poet before enlisting, and continued to write during the war. His poems became more and more dark and depressing as he began to think that the war was wrong. In 1917, in England after being wounded, he wrote a letter to the Times newspaper saying that he refused to return to the war because he thought the soldiers' suffering was unjust. He was running a terrible risk and was almost put on trial for his anti-war beliefs but instead he was sent to hospital to be treated for shell shock (which is now called post traumatic stress disorder). He did return to the war, and lived until 1967, remembered as one of the greatest poets of the 20th century.

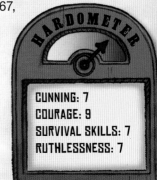

HARDOMETER

CUNNING: 7
COURAGE: 9
SURVIVAL SKILLS: 7
RUTHLESSNESS: 7

LAWRENCE OF ARABIA

HARD NUT RATING: 8.3

For hundreds of years, the Ottoman Empire ruled the Middle East from its capital at Constantinople (modern-day Istanbul in Turkey). By the time of the First World War, the empire was losing its grip, and in 1916 the Arab Revolt began against Ottoman rule.

GUERILLA WAR

The British were pleased that the Ottomans were fighting the Arabs because it stopped them from fighting the Allies. T E Lawrence was a British intelligence officer sent to help the Arabs. He spoke Arabic, and wholeheartedly agreed with the Arabs and their revolt. He became known as Lawrence of Arabia, and helped unite the Arabs into a fearsome guerrilla army. In 1917 the Arabs captured the city of Aqaba, a port on the Red Sea, and by 1918 Ottoman rule ended in the Middle East.

HARDOMETER

CUNNING: 8
COURAGE: 9
SURVIVAL SKILLS: 8
RUTHLESSNESS: 8

GRABBING ARABIA

Instead of ruling themselves, the Arab countries were divided up between Britain and France. Lawrence strongly disagreed with this, but he couldn't do a lot about it. Later he served in the Royal Air Force and was killed in a motorbike accident in 1935.

ATATURK

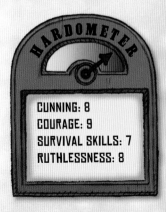

HARD NUT RATING: 8

Ataturk was born in the Ottoman Empire in what's now Greece. He went to military school, and served in the Ottoman Army, fighting against the Italians and in the Balkan Wars before the First World War. During the First World War, Ataturk became a war hero in the Dardanelles (a narrow sea dividing Europe and Asia), where he helped stop the Allied invasion in 1915.

INDEPENDENT TURKEY

After the war, the Ottoman Empire was broken up and the Allies began enthusiastically dividing up the land that used to be part of it. Ataturk demanded independence for Turkey, which wasn't what the Allies had in mind. He resisted attempts by Greece to grab land on Turkey's western coast, and finally established the Republic of Turkey. Ataturk was the country's first president, until he died in 1938. He was given the name Ataturk in 1935, which means Father of the Turks.

HARDOMETER

CUNNING: 8
COURAGE: 9
SURVIVAL SKILLS: 7
RUTHLESSNESS: 8

THE AMERICAN REVOLUTIONARY WAR

The British controlled quite a bit of North America, and wanted the American colonists to pay taxes to them. The Americans weren't so keen on the idea. In 1773, American traders emptied tons of British tea into the harbour at Boston, an event that became known as the Boston Tea Party, in protest against having to pay taxes on it.

THE PATRIOTS AND THE LOYALISTS

After the Boston Tea Party, the British sent troops to keep everyone in line. The American people split into patriots – anti-British – and loyalists – pro-British, and the French joined in on the side of the patriots. Eventually, the patriots won and British rule ended in 1783. The commander-in-chief of the patriots, George Washington, became the first president of the United States of America.

DEBORAH SAMPSON

HARD NUT RATING: 9.3

Deborah Sampson came from a poor family in Massachusetts, educated herself and worked as a teacher. But she really wanted to be a soldier, and the only way to do that was to disguise herself as a man. She enlisted in the patriot army as Robert Shurtleff without anyone guessing. The other soldiers called her Molly because she didn't have a beard, but they thought it was because she was a young boy, not a woman!

BATTLES AND RAIDS

Deborah might have fought in the siege of Yorktown in October 1781, the last major battle of the Revolution. The patriots were led by General George Washington, and, with some help from the French, they beat the British. Fighting continued after Yorktown, and Deborah was cut badly on her forehead and shot in her left thigh in a fight with loyalists. She had to hide the gunshot wound from the doctor and deal with it herself in case her disguise was discovered. While she was recovering she nursed a sick soldier in a private home – but the home turned out to belong to a loyalist, Van Tassel, who helped loyalist soldiers, and Deborah led a night raid on his house and captured 15 men.

WELL-KEPT SECRET

Deborah's true identity wasn't discovered until 1783, when she was honourably discharged. She married in 1785 and had three children.

HARDOMETER

CUNNING: 10
COURAGE: 10
SURVIVAL SKILLS: 9
RUTHLESSNESS: 8

THE KALINGA WAR

Indian hard nut Chandragupta conquered most of India and ruled the great Maurya Empire from 321 BC. A chunk of the south of India remained unconquered, and also a bit on the east coast – the republic of Kalinga.

TOP PRIORITY

Kalinga's coast line was handy for trading with countries further to the east, such as Burma, which made Kalinga rich. Chandragupta was probably quite annoyed that Kalinga remained outside his empire, especially since it had been part of a previous empire that Chandragupta had conquered. By the time his grandson, Ashoka the Great, became emperor of the Maurya Empire, conquering Kalinga had become a top priority.

ASHOKA THE GREAT

HARD NUT RATING: 6.3

Ashoka became emperor in 268 BC. He tried asking the Kalingan people nicely to become part of the Maurya Empire, but they refused. So, in 261 BC, Ashoka attacked.

BLOODY BATTLEFIELD

The Kalingan war proved to be extremely bloody. Ashoka attacked with 60,000 foot soldiers, 1,000 cavalry and 700 war elephants, but the Kalingan people fought back much harder than expected. At the end of it, 100,000 Kalingans were dead, including soldiers and civilians, and many more were taken prisoner. Ashoka's army suffered terrible losses too.

WAR AND PEACE

Ashoka had a reputation as a ruthless rampaging conqueror, but when he looked at the battlefield, littered with bodies, he decided never to fight again. Instead he changed his religion from Hinduism and became a Buddhist, which teaches non-violence. Ashoka became a peaceful vegetarian, and ordered his teachings to be carved on walls, rocks and huge decorated pillars, which were placed where lots of people would see them, and gave advice about how people should live good, moral lives. Despite his new outlook on life, he didn't give the Kalingans back their land – it became part of the Mauryan Empire, and stayed that way. Ashoka ruled peacefully until 232 BC.

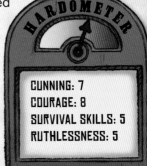

HARDOMETER

CUNNING: 7
COURAGE: 8
SURVIVAL SKILLS: 5
RUTHLESSNESS: 5

THE BATTLE OF THE ALAMO

The US state of Texas was part of Mexico in the early 1800s, which had been part of the Spanish Empire until it became independent in 1821. From the 1820s onwards, English-speaking people began to settle in Texas, and after a while it seemed like a good idea (to them at least) to be separate from the rest of Spanish-speaking Mexico. In 1835 Texans captured the town of San Antonio from the Mexicans.

ALAMO

Jim Bowie, one of the rebel Texan fighters, occupied a fort called the Alamo with a band of other armed rebels. They were joined by their leader William B Travis, and later by Davy Crockett. The Mexican Army of around 1,500 men, led by General Antonio López de Santa Anna, besieged the fort for 13 days, while Travis sent increasingly desperate messages for reinforcements. A hundred or so Texans arrived to help, but it wasn't enough. At dawn on 6 March 1836 the Mexicans attacked and broke into the fort, ruthlessly killing all of the 200 or so Texan rebels defending it. The Texans got their revenge a month later at the Battle of Jacinto, which ended the Texas Revolution.

DAVY CROCKETT

By the time of the Alamo, Davy Crockett was already well known as a tough, bear-grappling folk hero, straight-talking politician and charismatic storyteller. He was born in 1786 into a poor settler family in Tennessee, which at the time was the western frontier for the US settlers, a landscape that offered a good living for the settlers, but also dangers in the form of bears, mountain lions, venomous snakes and hostile Indians.

HARD NUT RATING: 7.3

TEXAN REBELS

Crockett made his reputation in the war against the Creek Indians in 1813-14 as a member of the Tennessee militia, then, despite his lack of education, he became a politician. He lost an election in 1835 and headed for Texas, fed up with politics, to fight with the rebels. The rebel Texans were overjoyed when he arrived at the Alamo fort. But even he couldn't win against overwhelming odds: he fought bravely, but was captured and killed by the Mexicans.

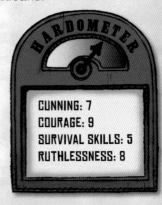

HARDOMETER

CUNNING: 7
COURAGE: 9
SURVIVAL SKILLS: 5
RUTHLESSNESS: 8

THE CRIMEAN WAR

In 1853, Tsar Nicholas of Russia attacked the weak Ottoman Empire, which was ruled from what's now Turkey and covered parts of the Middle East, North Africa and Europe. Britain and France didn't want Russia grabbing land and controlling their trade routes. The Ottomans were even less pleased about the situation, and fought back fiercely, but Russia gained some of the land that used to belong to the Ottomans.

HOME FOR TEA?

In 1854 Britain and France declared war on Russia. They planned to batter the Russians, win, then go home for tea. It didn't work out like that, though. The armies met on the Crimean peninsula, in what was then part of Ukraine (in 2014 Crimea became part of Russia again). The Crimean War went on until the spring of 1856, and involved major land battles and terrible loss of life: 25,000 British were killed, 100,000 French, and possibly up to a million Russians. But most of the soldiers didn't die in battle, they were killed by disease. Only one in six deaths in Crimean army hospitals were because of war wounds.

MARY SEACOLE

HARD NUT RATING: 8.3

Hospitals in the Crimea were overcrowded, disease-ridden, filthy, and short on supplies. Most patients (and some nurses) didn't stand much chance of getting out of them alive. Mary Seacole was born in Jamaica, which was part of the British Empire then, and was brave enough to apply to the British government volunteering as a nurse in the Crimea. Although the British sent Florence Nightingale and a team of trained nurses and nuns to the Crimea, they turned Mary Seacole down, even though she was experienced at treating cholera, the major killer in the Crimea.

BATTLEFIELD NURSING

Seacole was too tough to let that stop her. She went to the Crimea anyway, at her own expense, where she set up a hotel and shop, and used the profits to buy medicine to help battle-wounded soldiers. She even nursed injured soldiers on the battlefield. After the war she settled in Britain, where she became famous and was awarded medals by the British government, recognising her bravery and life-saving help.

HARDOMETER

CUNNING: 9
COURAGE: 10
SURVIVAL SKILLS: 9
RUTHLESSNESS: 5

THE BATTLE OF HASTINGS

The Battle of Hastings is one of the most famous battles in English history. William the conqueror was Duke of Normandy in northern France, and he couldn't help noticing that there was a whole country on the other side of the Channel ruled by a king, Edward the Confessor, who happened to be his cousin. King Edward promised to make William heir to the throne of England (or that's what William said, anyway). But when Edward died in 1066, Harold Godwinson was crowned the next king of England instead of William.

ONE DAY BATTLE

William was furious. He sailed across the Channel and invaded England with a large army, and started pillaging and building castles. King Harold marched to meet him. In October 1066, William and Harold met at the Battle of Hastings. The battle was fought over the course of a day, and as a result England ended up with a Norman king.

KING HAROLD

HARD NUT RATING: 7.8

Harold became Earl of Wessex when his father died in 1053, making him one of the most powerful men in England. When King Edward the Confessor died in 1066, Harold claimed that Edward had named him as heir to the throne (obviously, some people disagreed with him) and was crowned king.

BOTHERSOME BROTHER

The previous year, Harold had made a dangerous enemy: his own brother, Tostig. Harold had replaced him as Earl of Northumbria after a revolt, instead of supporting him. So Tostig joined forces with Harald Hardrada, King of Norway, who invaded. Harald Hardrada and Tostig fought Harold at the Battle of Stamford Bridge near York. Harold won, and both Hardrada and Tostig were killed. But then Harold had more bad news: he found out about William the Conqueror's invasion on the south coast of England. He had to march his battle-weary army hundreds of miles south to meet him.

LAST BATTLE

The Battle of Hastings was fought only 19 days after the Battle of Stamford Bridge. The fighting lasted all day, but Harold's tired army was defeated and Harold was killed (possibly by an arrow in the eye). William the Conqueror became King of England.

HARDOMETER

CUNNING: 7
COURAGE: 8
SURVIVAL SKILLS: 7
RUTHLESSNESS: 9

THE AMERICAN CIVIL WAR

In 1860, 11 of the southern United States formed their own government and called themselves the Confederate States of America.

SLAVERY

Their problem with the other states in the Union mainly concerned slavery: the new US president was Abraham Lincoln, who was in favour of getting rid of slavery altogether. The Confederate States were keen to keep slavery because of their plantations – huge farms that produced sugar, tobacco, cotton and other crops, and relied on slave labour. There weren't any plantations in the northern Union States, but slavery still existed there. As a whole country, the United States held the most slaves of any country in the world at the time.

ABRAHAM LINCOLN

CONFEDERATE SOLDIER

UNION SOLDIER

WAR BEGINS

The following year, civil war broke out when Confederate soldiers attacked Union soldiers in Charleston harbour, South Carolina. The Union had a bigger army than the Confederates, but at the beginning of the war the Confederates won major battles, thanks to the cunning tactics of General Robert E Lee. The civil war went on for four years, from 1861-65. Eventually, the Union won, but only after many thousands of soldiers died – 750,000 of them. Two hundred thousand African Americans fought in the Civil War, many of them ex-slaves.

ROBERT E LEE

HARD NUT RATING: 8

Lee was born into a posh family in Virginia, one of the 11 Confederate states. He went to military school, then fought for the United States Army in the Mexican War, where his general called him the best soldier he'd ever seen.

SWITCHING SIDES

When the civil war began, the army offered Lee the command of all the Union troops, but he refused. Instead he decided to fight for the southern states: he resigned from the United States Army and took command of Virginian troops.

He soon began winning battles against the Union army – in one of them, Chancellorsville in 1862, his soldiers were outnumbered by two to one, but he still won.

CONFEDERATE DEFEAT

The first big Confederate defeat was at the Battle of Gettysburg in 1863. The next year, Union general Ulysses S Grant began pushing his army south, and in the end Lee couldn't stop him. He surrendered to Grant in 1865.

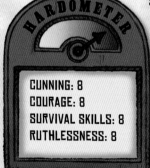

HARDOMETER

CUNNING: 8
COURAGE: 8
SURVIVAL SKILLS: 8
RUTHLESSNESS: 8

ROBERT E LEE

ULYSSES S GRANT

THE BATTLE OF ISANDLWANA

Towards the end of the 1800s Britain and other European countries were grabbing as much of Africa and its wealth as they could. By the 1870s, Britain controlled various bits of southern Africa, and wanted more – including the land of the Zulu people, who had very different ideas.

ZULULAND INVADED

In 1879, British troops launched an invasion of Zululand and started the Zulu War, which lasted about six months. The Battle of Isandlwana was its first battle, and ended in victory for the Zulus. On the same day as the Battle of Isandlwana, the Zulus attacked British soldiers at a settlement called Rorke's Drift. This time the British won, killing around 500 Zulu warriors. In the end the British won the war, and claimed Zululand for Britain – in 1897 it became part of the British colony of Natal, and today it's part of South Africa.

KING CETSHWAYO

HARD NUT RATING: 8.5

Cetshwayo became King of the Zulu in 1872 when his father, King Mpande, died.

PLANS FOR EXPANSION

The Zulus and the British had got along fairly well until the British, under Sir Bartle Frere, demanded that Cetshwayo give up his army and step down from power. Cetshwayo was not keen on the British expansion plans. Instead, he gathered his massive army (around 40,000 or more strong) and prepared for war.

DEFEATED

Cetshwayo led his troops to a hill called Isandlwana where British troops were camped. In a surprise attack the Zulu warriors killed about 1,350 of the 1,750 British soldiers defending it. Despite their victory at Isandlwana, the Zulus lost the war. Cetshwayo was captured by the British in August 1879 and imprisoned while Zululand was divided between the British and enemies of the Zulus. Later, Cetwshwayo travelled to London to meet Queen Victoria in an attempt to get his kingdom back, and he was given a small area of his old kingdom to rule in 1883. But a civil war broke out and Cetshwayo gave up ruling for good. He died suddenly the following year.

HARDOMETER

CUNNING: 9
COURAGE: 9
SURVIVAL SKILLS: 7
RUTHLESSNESS: 9

CUBAN REVOLUTION

In 1952 Fidel Castro stood for election as Cuba's president. It looked as though Castro would win, until the government was overthrown by General Fulgencio Batista, who took control and cancelled the election. Outraged, Castro and his brother Raul led a rebellion against Batista. It failed, and Castro was captured and imprisoned, but he was released two years later and ran away to Mexico, where he met Che Guevara.

SUCCESS

In 1956 Castro landed in Cuba with Guevara and the rest of his rebel band, and began to fight the government by guerrilla warfare. This time, Castro was successful: in 1959 Batista was forced to flee, and Castro became president. He got rid of Batista's unfair system, and Cuba became a communist country, where wealth is divided more equally and resources like farms, mines and factories are owned by the government instead of rich individuals. Cuba is still communist, and was ruled by Fidel Castro until he retired in 2008.

CHE GUEVARA

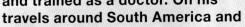

HARD NUT RATING: 7.8

Che Guevara is one of the most famous revolutionaries ever. He was born in Argentina in 1928 and trained as a doctor. On his travels around South America and North America (some of them by motorbike) he was horrified by the gap between rich and poor. He decided to try and do something about it, and believed the best method was armed revolution.

GUERILLA TACTICS

In 1955 he met Fidel Castro, enthusiastically joined his revolutionary group and fought bravely and cleverly in the guerrilla war in Cuba, on one occasion defeating government troops despite being outnumbered by eight to one. In 1959, when Castro became president of Cuba, Guevara was made president of the National Bank, and then Minister of Industry. But eventually he fell out with some of the other Cuban leaders and tried spreading revolution in Africa instead.

BOTHER IN BOLIVIA

Guevara's revolutionary plans didn't work out in Africa, so he returned to South America and trained rebel forces in Bolivia. The Bolivian Army, with help from the United States, captured and executed him. His body was buried in a secret location, but in 1997 it was discovered and reburied in Cuba.

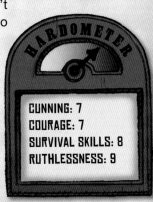

HARDOMETER

CUNNING: 7
COURAGE: 7
SURVIVAL SKILLS: 8
RUTHLESSNESS: 9

THE BATTLE OF BOYACÁ

At the beginning of the 1800s, some South Americans were getting fed up with being ruled by Spain, who had sent settlers to South America centuries before, and still hung on to the land and its wealth.

SURPRISE!

The leaders of these South American rebels, Simón Bolívar and Francisco de Paula Santander, marched their army on Bogotá, the capital of New Granada (today it's the capital of Colombia). The first battle against Spanish General Barreiro ended in a draw, but the second was much more successful for the rebels. A sneaky shortcut and an overnight march meant that the Spanish were taken by surprise, and on 7 August 1819 Bolívar and Santander led two rebel forces against a much larger Spanish Army. The Spanish were battered: there were more than 200 dead, and 1,600 taken prisoner. The battle was a turning point in the struggle for independence from Spain.

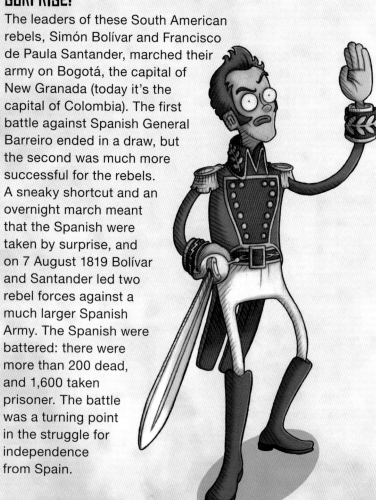

SIMÓN BOLÍVAR

HARD NUT RATING: 7.3

Bolívar was born in 1783 in Caracas, New Granada (modern-day Venezuela), into a wealthy family. He travelled to Europe, where he vowed to do something about independence for his country.

COLOMBIAN INDEPENDENCE

Bolívar went back to South America, and in 1810 Venezuela declared itself independent from Spain, but didn't stay that way for long. Bolívar fought for independence and got it, but once again it didn't last: in 1814 Spanish general Boves defeated Bolívar, and Bolívar fled to Jamaica. But he was soon back, this time to attack the capital of New Granada, Bogotá. After the Battle of Boyacá, Bolívar marched on to Bogotá, the Spanish officials fled, and the Republic of Colombia was created.

GRAN COLOMBIA

That just left the rest of South America to deal with. In 1821, Bolívar finally ousted the Spanish in Venezuela for good, and created Gran Colombia, with some help from the liberator of Argentina, San Martin. Bolívar had succeeded in kicking out the Spanish, but there was internal fighting in Gran Colombia. Eventually, in 1830, Bolívar resigned from his position as dictator of the country, and intended to go back to Europe, but he died of tuberculosis on the way (though some say he was poisoned).

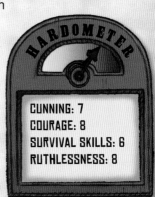

HARDOMETER

CUNNING: 7
COURAGE: 8
SURVIVAL SKILLS: 6
RUTHLESSNESS: 8

THE SECOND WORLD WAR

Twenty years after the end of the First World War, Europe was at it again – and this time it was on an even bigger scale. More than 70 million people died in the Second World War, the biggest armed conflict ever.

NAZIS, ALLIES AND AXIS

Adolf Hitler, leader of the Nazi party, ruled Germany from 1933, and began gathering a huge army and weapons for Germany, which broke the rules of a treaty signed after the First World War. In 1939 Germany invaded Poland, and Britain, and France declared war on Germany. On the side of the Allies were Britain, France and later the Soviet Union (after Germany invaded in 1941), the United States (after the US navy was bombed in 1941), plus a long list of other countries. The other side was the Axis – Germany, Japan (which had been at war with China since 1931) and Italy (which joined in 1940).

WAR FRONTS

The German Army occupied great chunks of Europe, and the Germans and the British bombed one another. The war was also fought in North Africa (because Libya was Italy's colony, and it's next to Egypt, which was protected by Britain), the Atlantic Ocean, where German submarines sank British supply ships, and Asia and the Pacific, where Japan was busy invading.

HOLOCAUST

One of the most terrible events in history happened during the Second World War – the Holocaust. Hitler wanted to get rid of Jewish people, and carried out orders for the mass killings of Jews, plus some other people he didn't like. They either executed them in gas chambers or sent them to labour camps where they were worked to death. Millions died in the Holocaust.

THE END OF THE WAR

In the first few years of the war it looked as though the Axis was winning: Germany captured France in 1940 and the Soviet Union in 1941, and Japan occupied large chunks of Asia. But by 1943 the Allies were doing much better, and in 1944 invaded and liberated France from the Germans. The Soviet Union drove the Germans out and invaded Germany. The war in Europe finally ended on 7 May 1945, and in Japan on 14 August 1945, after the United States dropped two nuclear bombs on Japan.

VIOLETTE SZABO

HARD NUT RATING: 9

Violette Szabo did one of the riskiest jobs of the Second World War: working undercover in German-occupied France.

SPECIAL OPERATIONS

After Germany invaded and occupied France in 1940, Britain set up the Special Operations Executive (SOE) to fight the Germans behind enemy lines by guerrilla warfare – blowing up bridges and trains, ambushing German troops, and using spies to find out what the Germans were up to. The brave men and women who worked undercover for the SOE knew that they were running huge risks, and stood a good chance of being executed if they were caught. They were all volunteers. One of them was Violette Szabo, who was 22 when the SOE approached her to work in France – she accepted straight away. Szabo had grown up in England and France, because her mother was French, and spoke French fluently. Her husband was a French officer who had been killed in North Africa in 1942, and they had a daughter.

MISSION IMPOSSIBLE

The SOE trained Szabo to use weapons and explosives, the art of disguise, and, among other things, how to derail a train, escape from handcuffs and use a parachute. While Szabo was busy learning all this she led a double life, and her family had no idea what she was up to. After parachuting into occupied territory on her second mission to France, she and a colleague were stopped at a German road block. Although she had the chance to run away, Szabo insisted that the other resistance fighter should escape, while, according to some reports, she gave him cover by shooting at the Germans until she was captured.

PRISON

Szabo was questioned by the Germans, and possibly tortured, and was eventually sent to prison in Germany, where conditions were terrible. A few months before the war ended, she was executed by firing squad with two other female spies, Denise Bloch and Lilian Rolfe. After her death she was awarded the George Cross by the British, the highest award for a civilian, and the Croix de Guerre and the Medaille de Resistance by the French.

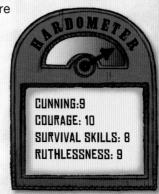

HARDOMETER

CUNNING: 9
COURAGE: 10
SURVIVAL SKILLS: 8
RUTHLESSNESS: 9

MORDECHAI ANIELEWICZ

HARD NUT RATING: 8.5

Mordechai Anielewicz was the leader of the largest armed resistance by Jews against the Nazis.

THE WARSAW GHETTO

Anielewicz was a Polish Jew – considering that the Nazis were against Jews and were about to invade Poland, this was a very bad position to be in. Just a week before the German invasion he managed to escape from his home in Warsaw. A third of the city's population was Jewish and the Nazis forced all 490,000 of them to live in one small part of the town – the Warsaw Ghetto. Food was scarce and lots of people starved or died of disease. Anielewicz had been planning to open an escape route to Palestine for Jews, but when his plans were thwarted he went back to Warsaw to help.

FIGHTING BACK

From 1942 to 1944 the Nazis sent the people of all Jewish ghettos to be executed. Many of the Jews from the Warsaw Ghetto had been sent to a death camp before Anielewicz and the other Jewish people found out about the mass killings. Although he was young, Anielewicz was a natural leader, incredibly brave and as hard as nails: he decided to fight back. He became leader of the Jewish Fighting Organisation, resisting the Nazis and smuggling in weapons.

HARDOMETER

CUNNING: 9
COURAGE: 9
SURVIVAL SKILLS: 6
RUTHLESSNESS: 10

When the Nazis came to transport more Jewish people in January 1943, they met armed men and women who put up a massive fight. Lots of the resistance fighters were killed, but they succeeded in stopping the transportation and driving out the Nazis . . . for a while.

LAST STAND

In April 1943 the Nazis were back. They sent tanks, artillery and planes to remove the remaining 50,000 or so Jews from the ghetto. The Jewish fighters were armed and barricaded themselves into buildings, preparing for the most desperate fight of their lives. Fighting raged in the streets for weeks, and the Nazis were driven back. But in the end, the Nazis' greater numbers and better weapons meant that almost all the resistance fighters in the ghetto were killed, including Anielewicz, who was just 23.

WARS AND BATTLES QUIZ

How much have you discovered about wars and battles, and the hard nuts who fought in them? Take this quiz and find out.

1. Which hard nut general was defeated by Julius Caesar in the Great Roman Civil War?

a) Crassus

b) Pompey

c) Sulla

2. Which of these South American countries is named after a revolutionary leader?

a) Colombia

b) Ecuador

c) Bolivia

3. Which Russian revolutionary was the leader of the Red Army in the Russian Civil War?

a) Leon Trotsky

b) Vladimir Lenin

c) Joseph Stalin

CRAZY HORSE

SITTING BULL

4. Queen Artemisia commanded a fleet of ships for . . . ?

a) The Greeks

b) The Romans

c) The Persians

5. Sitting Bull and Crazy Horse led Native American Indians into which of these battles?

a) The Little Big Horn

b) The Alamo

c) Gettysburg

6. Which of these British soldiers fought for the Serbian Army in the First World War?

a) Siegfried Sassoon

b) T E Lawrence

c) Flora Sandes

7. Which ruthless conqueror gave up conquering for a life of peace after the Kalinga War?

a) Chandragupta

b) Ashoka the Great

c) Aurangzeb

8. Who was defeated by William the Conqueror at the Battle of Hastings?

a) Harald Hardrada

b) Edward the Confessor

c) Harold Godwinson

9. Robert E Lee and Ulysses S Grant fought on opposing sides in which war?

a) The American Revolutionary War

b) The American Civil War

c) The Texas War of Independence

10. Che Guevara fought with Fidel Castro in a revolution in which country?

a) Cuba

b) Colombia

c) Costa Rica

11. Mary Seacole and Florence Nightingale nursed soldiers in which war?

a) The Second World War

b) The Napoleonic Wars

c) The Crimean war

12. The Battle of the Alamo was fought in which US state?

a) Texas

b) Virginia

c) Florida

13. Mordechai Anielewicz fought in the Second World War in the Jewish ghetto of which city?

a) Paris

b) Amsterdam

c) Warsaw

14. King Cetshwayo ruled which of these African peoples?

a) Ashanti

b) Zulu

c) Maasai

15. Which war started after the Boston Tea Party?

a) American Revolutionary War

b) American Civil War

c) English Civil War

Answers: 1b), 2c) – named after Simón Bolívar, 3a), 4c), 5a), 6c), 7b), 8c) 9b), 10a), 11c), 12a), 13c), 14b), 15a).

57

HARD NUT WARS AND BATTLES TIMELINE

480 BC

Battle of Salamis, a sea battle between the Greeks and the Persians. Queen Artemisia of Halicarnassus commanded five ships in the Persian fleet.

261 BC

The Kalinga War was fought in India. It was won by Ashoka the Great, and Kalinga became part of his empire.

49 BC

Start of the Great Roman Civil War, fought between Julius Caesar and the general Pompey the Great.

48 BC

Pompey was executed in Egypt.

44 BC

Julius Caesar was assassinated in Rome by a group of politicians.

C. 1020

Harold Godwinson was born. He became King of England in 1066 but was killed at the Battle of Hastings the same year.

1066

The Battle of Hastings was won by William the Conqueror, who became King of England.

1760

Deborah Sampson was born, and went on to fight in the American Revolutionary War disguised as a man.

1769

Hard nut British general the Duke of Wellington was born.

1773

The Boston Tea Party took place, when tonnes of British tea was dumped into Boston Harbour as a protest by the Americans at having to pay taxes to the British.

1775

The American Revolutionary War began. It ended in 1783 and so did British rule in America.

1783

Simón Bolívar, revolutionary South American leader, was born.

1786

American folk hero Davy Crockett was born.

1805

Mary Seacole, who became a nurse in the Crimean War, was born.

1807

Confederate general Robert E Lee was born.

1815

The Battle of Waterloo was fought between the French, led by Napoleon, and the British and their allies, led by the Duke of Wellington.

1819

The Battle of Boyacá was fought, a turning point in South America's battle for independence from Spain.

1821

French general and emperor Napoleon died in exile.

1836

The Battle of the Alamo was fought between Texan rebels and Mexico.

1854

The Crimean War, fought between allies Britain and France against Russia.

1861

Start of the US Civil War, which finally ended in 1865.

1872

Cetshwayo became King of the Zulu.

1876

The Battle of the Little Bighorn, fought between the US Army and an army of united Native American tribes. It ended with the death of General Custer and most of his troops.

1876

Flora Sandes was born. She fought in the Serbian Army in the First World War.

1879

Russian revolutionary Leon Trotsky was born.

1879

Battle of Isandlwana, fought between the British and the Zulu in Africa.

1881

Ataturk was born. He fought in the First World War and made Turkey an independent country.

1886

Siegfried Sassoon, soldier in the First World War and poet, was born.

1888

T E Lawrence was born. He became known as Lawrence of Arabia because he helped organise the Arab Revolt during the First World War.

1914

Start of the First World War, which went on until 1918.

1917

The Russian Revolution, which ended with the Bolshevik Party in power.

1919

Mordechai Anielewicz was born, leader of the Jewish uprising in Warsaw during the Second World War.

1921

Violette Szabo was born. During the Second World War she was sent into Occupied France as a British Special Operations Executive, and was caught and executed.

1928

Revolutionary Che Guevara was born.

1939

Outbreak of the Second World War, the biggest war there's ever been.

1959

Fidel Castro led the Cuban Revolution and became the country's president.

1965

Start of the Vietnam War, fought between the United States and Vietnam. It continued until 1973.

GLOSSARY

ALLIANCE an agreement between different countries or nations to work together in order to achieve something

ASSASSINATED killed for political reasons

BANISHED sent away and banned from returning

BESIEGED surrounded by enemy forces

CAVALRY soldiers on horseback

CHOLERA often fatal disease caught from dirty water

CIVIL WAR war between groups of people from the same country or state

COLONISTS people who settle in another country or region and take control of it

COMMUNIST someone who believes in a system based on common ownership

CONSUL a leader of the Roman Empire

DICTATOR a leader who takes total power and authority

EXILED banned from your native country

GHETTO an area of a city to which Jews were restricted to live

GUERRILLA small independent group fighting

GUILLOTINE a large machine used to behead people

HAND GRENADE a small bomb that can be thrown by hand

MILITIA an army made up of ordinary people rather than professional soldiers

PLANTATION a huge farm on which crops such as coffee, sugar and tobacco are grown

REBELS people who break away from (or resist) authority

REPUBLIC a state in which the people elect the leaders, and that has a president rather than a king or queen

REVOLUTION an overthrow of a leader

SENATE the Roman government

SETTLERS people who move to a new country or region and set up home there permanently

SHELL SHOCK suffering from symptoms such as depression and flashbacks due to traumatic experiences; now called post traumatic stress disorder

TUBERCULOSIS a lung disease that can be fatal

INDEX